I0626420

Feathered Throat

by

Allisonn Church

Crooked Circle Press

Bailey, CO / 2025

CROOKED CIRCLE PRESS

ISBN: 979-8-9888904-4-7

First Edition

To a woman I hardly know

Contents

Dwelling

What memories haunt
the caverns of this body?
Dig deep and find them…

Anatomy Gone Mad

> *"I know where lodges the heart in others.*
> *In the breast— as everyone knows!*
> *But with me*
> *anatomy has gone mad:*
> *nothing but heart*
> *roaring everywhere."*
> *— Vladimir Mayakovsky,*
> *translated by Max Hayward and George Reavey*

My heart has four chambers (which is to say, rooms):
my entire body fits inside one of them; my thoughts,
another; the largest room houses a map of the world,
full scale; there is a fourth room, but I've never seen it.

Whenever I fall in love (which is often, daily or more),
my heart constricts 'til it can slip in my beloved's pocket,
or an envelope to mail. It is a painful process—
though my heart has no bones, somehow

it manages to break
each time.

Thursday's Child

When I was born, the moon was in Sagittarius.
She attempted to free the stars
from their dark vault, but
most remained in constellation
(dutiful beings as they are).

A cluster of wayward stars leapt at the call
descending to Earth in glittering avalanche,
white hot sparks dappling my cheeks,
my chest, my left shoulder.

Now I turn my face to the moon and remember
how she once marked me for freedom.

Ghost

I hope to fool you into believing
I am a ghost—

appearing as if from autumn air,
a sudden leaf;

dissolving
into campfire smoke.

Survival of a Winged Skeleton

When I was young, I was a bird: I rose at dawn and perched in treetops; my bones were hollow. Nobody knew what sort of bird I was, and everyone else was human. It was tricky, but I loved myself anyway; I loved the brisk rush of March wind rustling my lush feathers.

When I grew larger, and larger still, people gawked. I wasn't shaped right, they said— my bones, too cavernous. They cackled and hissed, and their words sunk deep into the open pockets of my buoyant wrists, my thick, porous ankles. Soon my bones were so full of bad words that I could no longer fly: my skeleton had collapsed beneath the weight.

Grief-stricken, I plucked out all my feathers until I was nothing but pale skin and flat feet. I walked the earth that way for decades, always gazing up at the clouds. One morning, in the company of two white hens, a tender voice on the March breeze whispered, "open."

I sucked the crisp dawn air into my bones and ascended an oak branch, casting a massive shadow. With the quickening branch clutched in my newly sharpened claws, I called down to my shadow, "You deserve to be happy."

Something Else

I'm a nice person and a liar—
do with that what you will.

You'd think my heart knows,
      my soul knows,
her own truth,
      but there are clouds
even under my skin;
        there are silver clouds....

A Vacancy

The sky falls in September,
hard and loud through the oak leaves.

We cover our heads while the fruit plummets
to the earth, and everyone we know leaves.

We are alone in the forest. We always wanted
this: a silent house. A curl of smoke leaves

the chimney and hangs in the branches:
what else will we have when this hope leaves?

Reciprocity

Birds bursting from trees, settling
in trees, fluttering under clouds.
Birds, fluffed and feathery, preening
in puddles, in bundles and bands
near the roadside. Birds calling:
catbirds and crows, blue jays
and broad-winged hawks; each breath
from my wondering lungs
rises to lift their wings.

Spring

Robins have overtaken
front yard and crabapple—
a welcome invasion.

I cede this land to their hunger,
copper bellies,
rain cloud wings.

Ghost

Leaves dance in the wind,
a faint ghost of the moon floats
on a blue sky sea

After "Meditations in an Emergency"

We place heaven in the sky where there are no borders,
only wind. We pray that those who die needlessly
in war ascend somewhere limitless. We pray
to the golden dawn, lit with fire. We pray
to the legion of stars.

Flight

In the beginning, Earth was an endless ocean
and I was a bird—

I know this is true
because I never could have survived
the depths of that tremendous sea,
but today the ghosts of primal winds
ruffle my dormant flight feathers.

My son wonders what creatures
lurk in dark water,
but I fixate instead
on the fiery sun,
prepared to raise my shrill voice
to the sky and follow it
beyond all horizons.

Break

Life at the end of the world
         cuts me open,
like a sharp beak with a seed

Rural Summer

My son holds a piece of sugary red candy out the car window— he says, "I'm getting the taste of the air." We follow the curving river, near flood stage in July, flanked by soggy corn fields. A killdeer here, a heron there, feathers rising from maple branches. Feathers caressing warm air like red candy. Feathers in barns, more colorful than the old graffiti, brighter than green tobacco leaves. Feathers clinging to the sticky mess of my son's fingers. When he leans out the window just a little bit further, I know he will fly away.

Originally published in "Iceberg's Poetry" on Medium.com

Offering

I gather sturdy stalks of joy bedecked
with indefatigable blossoms—
arrange a lively bouquet
of confidently offbeat aspirations
in a basket woven from spider silk
and frail hope.

I take it to the grave.

A Blossom

When paperwhites bloom,
you could choke on the sweetness
and cough up honey.

A Breath

Day of the full moon—
I watch the purple hostas
that move on whispers.

Morning Chores

In the morning I hear angels
ringing in my ears; I tune them out,
close my eyes and find an owl
watching. I walk
to the coop— one white bird
stretches a feathered wing
like an angel.

And the morning sun floats
through paper-thin fog
becoming something
else.

I see the angels' breath now,
caught in dewdrops— everywhere.
And a crowd of flowers
bent to the earth
as if in prayer.

The Jar

I open my mouth to the mirror and see
a swollen tongue stuck in my throat; reach in
and extract a fistful of spiders
and stars. They drip down my chin:
streams of spiders escape my esophagus,
silver sparks ricochet from my lungs.

I gather them all together with fumbling hands,
collect them in a jar, place the jar on the floor
of my closet beneath an old sweater,
tuck myself in to sleep.

As I rest, the stars in my closet whisper and pulse
in conversation with the night sky.
A single strand of silk clings to my lungs,
threading its way to a tired spinneret
huddled in the dark.

Ghost

We sit at the dining table,
discussing memories and ghosts
while two women in elaborate gowns
sip tea in the living room

and whisper. A man in a top hat
patrols the hall. My mother-in-law
talks about the dirt floor basement
of her childhood home—
unearthed treasures, shattered glasses,
empty picture frames, repeating dreams.

I try to memorize the glass cabinets,
the pots hanging on the wall
by the window. I think this memory
could be a ghost.

Inner Child Meditation

The dread inside my chest spreads like wet paint until
it bleeds into a cloudless sky, until I choke and sputter
on stars, throat closed around midnight. I rest a palm
against my breast bone, trying to ease the knot, when
my finger finds a small feather growing there. Through
rasps and rattles of strained breath, I remember when
I was a young bird, perched in my parents' willow, feel-
ing the wind. My hair was dull straw— the kind Rum-
pelstiltskin wished spun into gold. It was straw caked
in cow shit. It was a barn floor. My mouth, my cheeks
smeared in mud. Unaware of my own monstrosity, I
climbed branches like King Kong clambering up the
Empire State. I surveyed the land, feeling myself a
titmouse while the neighbors saw vulture— wild and
bloody, waiting to feast on their dead.

Prayer to My Turkey Vulture Tattoo

Dear Maude,

Guide my path
as I scour this landscape of rot and decay.
Help me find peace and redemption
in a blood-spattered wasteland. Help me
swallow the good bits whole.

Let the lump in my throat be the discarded corpse
of my worst nightmares, that it may dissolve
in the sharp acid pit of my ribs,
that I may cough up its bones and spit
frail hope into the chill winter air.

Originally published in "The Crooked Circle" on Medium.com

Prayer for Being

Lord, remind me
to hold fast
to the real world

(where real means
flesh & bone,
teeth & tongue).

Behind, around,
beneath these bones,
this tongue,

there is a light,
all the light,
invisible to bones.

The Healing

Soft light, soft chair, soft candles
with their gentle glow— the trickle
of a tabletop fountain. My therapist

arranges space and time to a theme
of sanctuary. I close my eyes, examine
the cells of my human body, suspended

here, between earth and sky. Just there,
in the basin between clavicles, something
sticks. I open my mouth wide, gather

the full force of my breath, exhale,
hoping to expel the blockage. I choke
on a lump of rotting flesh— not mine—

something animal, other. Flies swarm,
hungry for death; blood sprays, blood
drips down my chin as I cough—

I am losing my breath. The primal matter
is stuck. Buzzing insects throb; my eyes
shake in their sockets; a hand grasps

at my throat. Unable to expel this thing,
unable to swallow it, I collapse in a pile
of bones on the office floor. The flies

do their work, busy mouths breaking down
the morbid flesh. And I fall asleep
to their humming. And I awaken again,

hours later, having driven myself home.

Eiderdown

When my heart opens,
feathers pour out, float skyward,
kiss the open air…

Eating the Flowers on
My Grandparents' Grave

Barefoot in the cool cemetery grass, we walk
between corn stalks and clouds, tracing shadows
all the way to this final resting place.
My aunt has planted nasturtiums,
spicy and vibrant, in the hollow log
that lives here. We read the names, the dates—
we reach beneath the flat green umbrellas
and pluck two flowers.
My son gobbles his up whole.

　　　　He says the spice is not too much.
　　　　　　He says *this is good*.

We leave,
and the flowers keep blooming.

Originally published in "Sunlight Leaking" from Bottlecap Press

To My Son

Inside your lost molar,
a miniature sea scallop,
a ghost of your past life,
when you belonged to the sea.

How many ocean creatures
nestle against your jawbone
that you speak of streams
and rain with such tenderness?

Ghost

I feed my soul live crickets
in summertime; I pin her
between my tongue and the roof
of my mouth
so she won't escape.

She is the shape of trees
drowning in gold light,
warm sun spilling between
nascent branches— even now,
she haunts you.

www.ingramcontent.com/pod-product-compliance
Lightning Source LLC
Chambersburg PA
CBHW051651120626
46551CB00015B/2313